I0817038

EARTH'S ENERGY RESOURCES

# OIL ENERGY

ELSIE OLSON

Consulting Editor, Diane Craig, M.A./Reading Specialist

Sandcastle

An Imprint of Abdo Publishing
abdopublishing.com

abdopublishing.com

Published by Abdo Publishing, a division of ABDO, PO Box 398166, Minneapolis, Minnesota 55439. 

Printed in the United States of America, North Mankato, Minnesota

052018
092018

Design and Production: Mighty Media, Inc.
Editor: Liz Salzmann
Cover Photographs: Shutterstock
Interior Photographs: iStockphoto, Shutterstock, Wikimedia Commons

Library of Congress Control Number: 2017961702

**Publisher's Cataloging-in-Publication Data**
Name: Olson, Elsie, author.
Title: Oil energy / by Elsie Olson.
Description: Minneapolis, Minnesota : Abdo Publishing, 2019. | Series: Earth's energy resources
Identifiers: ISBN 9781532115554 (lib.bdg.) | ISBN 9781532156274 (ebook)
Subjects: LCSH: Petroleum as fuel--Juvenile literature. | Power resources--Juvenile literature. | Petroleum--Prospecting--Juvenile literature. | Energy harvesting--Juvenile literature. | Energy development--Juvenile literature.
Classification: DDC 553.28--dc23

## SandCastle™ Level: Fluent

SandCastle™ books are created by a team of professional educators, reading specialists, and content developers around five essential components—phonemic awareness, phonics, vocabulary, text comprehension, and fluency—to assist young readers as they develop reading skills and strategies and increase their general knowledge. All books are written, reviewed, and leveled for guided reading, early reading intervention, and Accelerated Reader™ programs for use in shared, guided, and independent reading and writing activities to support a balanced approach to literacy instruction. The SandCastle™ series has four levels that correspond to early literacy development. The levels are provided to help teachers and parents select appropriate books for young readers.

**EMERGING · BEGINNING · TRANSITIONAL · FLUENT**

# CONTENTS

All About Oil Energy 4

Think About It 22

Glossary 24

## ALL ABOUT OIL ENERGY

We use energy each day!

It comes from many **sources**. Oil is one source. It is a **fossil fuel**.

Oil formed from dead plants and animals in **swamps**.

Heat and **pressure** turned their remains to oil. This took millions of years.

People dig wells to get oil. Machines **pump** oil out of the wells.

Some drills dig under the ocean floor.

People discovered oil thousands of years ago.

But it wasn't commonly used until the 1800s. Oil lit lamps.

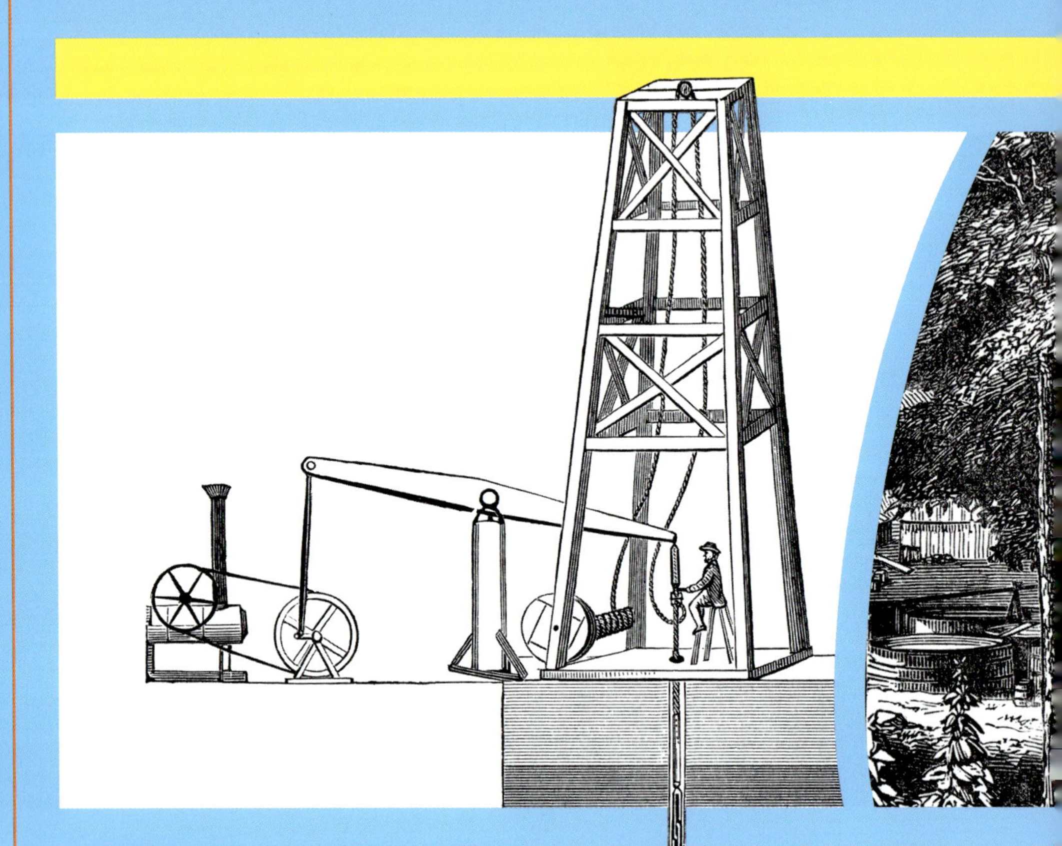

In 1859 Edwin Drake drilled the first US oil well.

Oil quickly became an important US **resource**.

Today we use oil to heat buildings.

Power plants burn oil to create electricity.

Factories **refine** oil. They turn it into gas. This powers cars.

Burning oil creates pollution.

Sometimes oil spills from oil wells. This harms the **environment**.

Scientists are working on these problems.

They try to prevent oil spills. They make cars that use less oil.

## THINK ABOUT IT

**Have you used oil energy? What did you use it for?**

# GLOSSARY

**environment** – nature and everything in it, such as the land, sea, and air.

**fossil fuel** – a fuel formed from the remains of plants or animals. Coal, oil, and natural gas are fossil fuels.

**pressure** – the force of something pressing against something else.

**pump** – to move a liquid or a gas through a tube or a pipe.

**refine** – to remove the unwanted substances from something.

**resource** – something that is usable or valuable.

**source** – where something comes from or begins.

**swamp** – an area of wet land often partly covered with water.